The Comeback

There is a rule that before getting a new book, one should read an old classic yet, as an author, I should not recommend too strict on adherence to his rule.

Winston Churchill

Table of contents:

We can never tell what is in store for us.

Harry S. Truman

Introduction:

You can be on top of the world, doing what you're programmed to accomplish. The world is yours. In a flash, that can all end as you get shattered by a stunning life-changer. In my case, it was meingitis. It can also be its cousin, a stroke. The dropoff from the mountain to the depths of a canyon or hell trips the circuit breaker off. Then, it's time to assess your position and your reserve of mental and physical horse power, deciding if you want to scrabble your way slowly out of the abyss. You can do it if you really crave it, and you need a stout team of doctors, thereapists, family and friends.

What a Journey and a Comeback you can mount!

Part 1:

Meningitis

In September, 1992, Peggy and I were in Ireland with Mr. And Mrs. Paul and George Hanley, two of our dearest friends. My sinus headaches were kicking up pretty badly, and my ENT doctor, a good one, had practically insisted on surgery for the next month as the only realistic solution for my sinusitis. Throughout our vacation, I felt a tickle of warning....

Meningitis .... Round One

I checked into an outpatient surgical center for my routine sinus surgery. Throughout my light sedation, I could hear my jocular surgeons chatting about comical dimensions in life as they rooted around my nasal cavities.

Apparently, during the course of the event one of them punctured the Cribifrom Plate at the top of my sinus, leading to a slight leak of my cerebral spinal fluid (CSF). According to conventional wisdom, that leak allowed an infection to spread through the subdermal section of my brain. Rocketing along, this germal chaos raced through my dura, or right frontal brain lining along the inside of my skull.

After my sinus surgery, I spent a hauntingly brief time in the recovery room, then haltingly made my way to my wife's car. We drove home and I sat in our family room with our eagerly attentive home-schooled children. After an hour or two I queerly felt a fever build, along with a sore neck. Down deep, I knew it wasn't right. Being tough, I ignored it, quietly getting scared. This could not be happening! It got worse and, finally, knowing there was something amiss, my wife called my ENT/surgeon to inquire about my developing symptoms. He asked me to head to the Froedtert Hosptial (Milwaukee's largest teaching hosptial) emergency room, where I'd be met by neurosurgeon, Dr. Glenn Meyers. My sense of panic mounted with my headache.

At Froedtert Hospital, I was given an MRI, then spoke with Dr. Glenn Meyer, who cooly told me that I would have to be admitted and watched. I checked into the Neurology floor, headache and fever still rising along with my befuddling panic. After being organized by the nurses, I began to note my surroundings. Since this was a teaching hosptial and the largest in the state, the quantity and quality of diverse neurological cases was endless. Periodically, I heard the shuffle of chains as orange-clad convicts seethingly were escorted down the hallway, often by deputies.

My headaches intensified, becoming almost unbearable. Movement and sound practically killed me, despite ice packs and merciful pain-killing injections every three hours. As the shots wore off, my headaches returned with crunching veangeance, and

I found myself timing each injection, eagerly awaiting the blessed relief it brought.

Across the hall from me was a hispanic fellow who had apparently gone through the windshild of his car while eluding pursuing authorities. The poor fellow would pour forth torrents of Spanish until a sympathetic nurse would, in a spasm of sympathy, misery and empathy, inject him with some palliative. His rantings would drift off over a minute or so, then cease for a few hours until the medicine wore off.

One night was particually poignant for me. To take pressure off my sinus damage point and to allow it to heal, Dr. Meyer drew off my excess cerebrospinal fluid via a spinal tap. As this was completed my headache pain exploded exponentially and became literally unbearable. That night, the lights were off on the floor and it was so dark that I could barely see my hand in front of my face. My pain injections were doing practically nothing to mitigate my screaming headache. Periodically, the prisoner across the hall would split the night with his hysterical incantations. The room's darkness pressed on me further, and I felt a gripping fear for my life. Could I handle this pain? Was this dying? What about losing my soulmate Peggy and my precious kids? I couldn't leave them! Could I handle this pain? Was this THE END I had read about? Suddenly, I knew I was being held by something brilliant-in bright, shining robes. I was being held like a baby, and felt a sense of total peace, of lightness. My headache evaporated and I felt at ease. The wild ravings across the hall stopped. Everything was well, and I fell into a profoundly blessed sleep.

I awoke in the morning refreshed and mystified to be alive after such a deeply moving experience. Within the next few days, the source of my first meningitis infection, the puncture from my surgery, closed itself. My first brush with meningitis was over, although my headaches still plague me to this day.

Luckily, I was now able to jump back into the middle of my Type-A life. During those few days in the hosptial, I had missed my wonderful wife and four children terribly, and I now took on new appreciation of our home-schooling activities. I was able to return, civically, to my weekly activities at Milwaukee's Rotary Club, of which I had previously been president. I was active in the Greater Milwaukee Committee (the dynamic shaper of Milwaukee's future), the Young Presidents' Organization, the Zoological Society of Milwaukee County (of which I was Chairman) and the Confrerie des Chevaliers du Tastevin (Burgundy wine society-my passion!). I was deeply religious, and remain so. And I was vigorously attacking tennis, paddle tennis and swimming with gusto.

I was the third generation owner of Heinemann's, a group of restaurants orginally founded by my grandfather in 1923. The pace has always been brutal, margins have always been slim and we'd been on an aggressive growth pace over the past twenty years.

There has always been too much going on in my life, too quickly and with too much pressure. I was too important, too busy, to be sick again...

In May, 1996, as Chairman of the Zoological Society of Milwaukee County, I was in the midst of Kissinger-like maneuverings to help ward off a looming financial crisis for Milwaukee's terrific zoo. Publicly supported, it simply could not afford to feasibly continue along its historical, financial and management model. Something had to give, and we were delicatley trying to step up to the plate to steer the operation into the next millennium. I spent aggressive weekends working on our farm, mainly with trees, but also installing a post fence for Peggy's new horse.

On May 8th, I felt sick at work, slightly dizzy with a splitting headache. "Forge on!" I said, with my typical do-or-die attitude, knowing I had to go to a black tie dinner that night with the French burgundy wine group that I so dearly loved. I figured it as merely a flu bug, as I visited the lofty offices of our friend and lawyer, Bill Abraham. My wrenching headache didn't yield to aspirin, and my temperature at home before I changed my clothes was 100.2 degrees. During our car trip to dinner I knew I was in trouble, and I felt more dizzy. At dinner I engaged in my typically light-spirited debates with Dr. Robert Condon, another burgundy lover who tended to, like me, be more vociferous than most. All the while, my spirits continued to sink as my dizziness and befuddlement grew. At dinner's end, I asked our car driver to drop me off first at home in advance of my fellow riders, as I could barely hold my head up straight. Things were not good. After I hesitantly made my way up the stairs to our bedroom, Peggy, with great concern, watched me crawl into bed miserably at 10:30pm. Normally, after a high-spirited night of drinking burgundy and debating its merits, I would stumble home singing my love for her. I stayed in bed.

On Friday morning, Peggy took my temperature and it had rocketed to 103.2, and she was getting alarmed. I said my head simply hurt too much to continue, as I was dizzy and nauseous. Concerned questions were handled with great difficulty.

I put one of my pain pills into my mouth, staring vacantly as it sat on my tongue. Finally, my family got me to swallow it, and louder alarm bells began sounding in Peggy's head. I went back to bed, with Peggy leaving me a can of soda and remonstrating me to drink. An hour later I was snoring and never awakened when Peggy came in to set her hair. I hadn't touched my soda. She left me alone, returning a couple of hours later after assuming that I simply needed sleep. She raised me, and my response was very slow. Her quiet alarm bells grew in intensity. At 5:00pm, I was still snoring, so she got our son, Johnny, to help wake me in order to determine whether or not to call our doctor. They unsteadily put me on the toilet, can of soda in hand, to see if I had to go to the bathrooom. I remember helplessly watching the can slip through my hand and onto the floor. I was absolutely powerless to hold it! My doctor told Peggy to take me to the emergency room of his practicing hospital (Columbia).

Peggy and Johnny tried to juggle dressing me, with farming out our smaller kids to friends and neighbors for safekeeping. As I was trundled into the car, I told Peggy that I really needed a Tylenol 4 (a gonzo pain reliever) for pain. Clearly alarmed, she hustled me to the hosptial.

At Columbia Hospital I was spirited away, and Peggy was told to stay in the waiting room. After ten minutes, she told the receptionist that the doctor may need her to relate what happened, since my communication skills at that point were practically nil. The doctor asked her to recapitulate the details for the past few days, then went to the CT scan room to await results.

The neurologist and neurosurgeon were terribly concerned with the swelling of my infected brain and they drilled four "burr holes" in my skull to relieve the pressure. Things immediately looked better and they kept me in the hospital for observation. After a few days I began heading south, and they sawed off a patch of my skull, watching my swollen brain pop out of my head. This prompted my doctors to plug me with tubes galore and lay me on a cooling pad to drop my temperature, all the while pumping me with antibiotics, realizing that death was a real possibility.

In 1952, my mother fed me a hard boiled egg, the yolk of which I quickly inhaled, choking and turning purple. Her own version of a Hemlich Maneuver saved me, but I retained a loathing of all things yolky there after. As I recovered from my two surgeries, a kind nurse lightly poached an egg to provide needed nutrition. Naturally I started gagging uncontrollably, scaring the pants off the staff. They almost called for a code cart.

Additionally, my sister brought me some freshly squeezed orange juice to comfort my scathing throat after I had borne an assocrtment of breathing tubes. While she was visiting, I chanced a look at a mirror and recoiled in horror. I was beholding a visage of a half-shaven head, swollen brain and tubes. "I can't go to work like this tomorrow!", I moaned. Given what I'd been through, that was the least of my problems.

In the meantime, Peggy fended off visiting, concerned friends and waited for her mother to appear. When she did, Peggy collapsed into her arms, sobbing uncontrollably. In the meantime, I slipped into a coma, decorated with my array of tubes, IV, etc. I didn't look terribly attractive with my swollen open brain, etc. Horror movie time... my coma lasted 17 days and drew a score of concerned people calling on the phone, proferring prayers and prepping fortifying meals for my family. Two neurosurgeries later and out of an abundance of panicked, concern and caution, Peggy made her call.

Faces, gurneys, rosaries, MRIs, oxygen tubes, hideous pain, crying, morphine, two surgeries, inky dreams, bloody stools, quickly composed songs, my best-friend priest, Bob Massey, reacting in shock to the horrific splendor of this near corps loaded with tubes and devices, seizures, etc. Drills, quiet voices, surgical suites, hand-holding, incantations to "hold on!", darkness, peace including those 17 days in a coma. It was a dark and agonizing time with a huge dollop of confusion and pain. Great friend Brian Nahey brought in a consulting neurologist from the University of Wisconsin hospital in Madison. Finally, in abject misery and humility over a condition that couldn't be lower, I begged Peggy to get me out of the hospital, or to transfer me to another. The poor dear blankly looked at me in practically stark terror, finally complying.

Froedtert neurosurgeon Dr. Glenn Meyer was called in to consult and, realizing the gravity of my condition, insisted on my transfer to Froedtert Hospital immediately. I faced immediate and imminent death without prompt surgery at Milwaukee's premier teaching hospital, he said. Amid vociferous complaints from the other hospital, I was bundled off into an ambulance for a trip to Froedtert and one more brain surgery, then darkness and more coma in the neuorlogy intensive care unit.

More darkness. More faces. More of my murky friend morphine. Quiet conversation of nurses and doctors on the Neurological floor. Brisk attentiveness of nurses. Still concerned, Dr. Meyer enlarged my skull bone flap.

Then, one of the major events in my life at that point took place. I awoke to the rustle of cloth and found my visitor to be a nurse. Through my haze I clearly saw her face and heard her voice,

"You'll never walk again!".

With that rocking pronouncement, she left me. Screaming rage rocketed up within me at her dooming sentence. How could I never walk? How could she? Why would she say such a thing? Why condemn a man so brutally? Given my nature, I even moved up in bed in an attempt to leap up and catch up with her.

I couldn't get up! I couldn't catch up with the moster! I could barely move! My right arm and leg could lash out in protest, but my left limbs were virtually powerless! I was stuck! How humbling! Here I was-weeks ago a vital, driven, dynamic man – and today, powerless and mocked. Her words, as unfair as they were, would prove to be my greatest motivation for the next four years.

The Comeback Begins

After the neuro floor, I was transferred to the Rehab wing of the hospital. Next to my bed as it was wheeled there, an assistant trolled a cart full of flowers and cards. It looked like a potential funeral procession, or at least smelled like it. As I was briskly settled into my new home, I realized that, in that area, a number of patients with sundry head injuries were residing. Nights were often punctuated with bizarre outbursts of moaning and screaming. On more than one occasion, I had to yell out for a particularly expressive patient to back off. Gosh – I thought, this is a hideous, earthly form of purgatory. I gained tremendous respect for the nuring staff.

One night I looked out into the corridor to see a man, totally nude, walking down the hall with a bombed-out look on his face, his hair totally disheveled. I had a haunting feeling I would see him again, and I found out from the nurses that his name was James. That night, I heard that one of the patients had left the ward and had taken the elvator down to the street. He travelled many blocks before his baffling presence was noticed and he was returned to the ward.

The next night, sure enough, my chilling foreshadowing was rewarded. When the lights were out, all was hair-raisingly dark, I felt a prescence in my room and heard a shuffling as a shadowy person, presumably a nurse, approached my bed. By now, I was well-used to nurses constantly changing the antibiotics on my I.V., so I didn't give it a second thought. I did when the bed sagged deeply as this person got into bed with me and, wide-eyed in the blackness, I was barely able to discern a pair of legs. To my chagrin, they were hairy! I then realized, with a sinking feeling of horror, that James was in bed with me and I had to quickly regroup to defuse a most awkward dilemma (to say the least).

"James" I said, "what do you think of the food here?" Silence. "How about them Brewers?" More grisly silence. I figured he was in the first deliberative stage of maiming or dismembering me. What a way to go after having gotten this far! In mounting panic, I figured that if I kept repeating his name at an attempt at conversation, some responsible nurse was bound to come to my aide before I bled to death. Luckily that happened and I didn't see

James until a number of weeks later.

Hospital Rehab Begins

My first rehab sessions started shortly thereafter, and I met

Michele Stamn. She took one look at my leg and the state of my

27

lack of mobility, sighed and got to work. A tough egg for a physical therapist, Michele literally had to move my leg manually as I stood up, with another therapist holding my right arm for balance so I could move my right leg. I worked with Michele twice per day, usually looking forward to our sessions with sinking inevitability, finishing them with marvelous relief. Nights brought exhaustion tinged with a good hurt in my leg, a hurt born of reactivation. Every morning began at 6:00am with a tender communion visit from the hospital's saintly Father Jerry. Then it was on to breakfast and rehab, then lunch, a rest, and more rehab. It began to dawn on my early on that this battle would be a matter of prayer and persistence.

Nurses, we all know, can make a hospital stay murky or brilliant, and I was blessed with the upbeat, positive Lynn Rasmussen. Her bubbly dynamism helped enormously, as did her unflagging faith in me, which she broadcast in every sinew. At one point, she told one of my best friends, Jim Taylor, that even though things looked bleak for me, she KNEW I would walk again. That buoyancy helped Jim's support of me immensely. In any great effort, especially rehab, a great support network is essential. Family, good friends, nurses and therapists are not only good – they're imperative. I kept in touch with Lynn practically monthly after leaving the hospital.

Great friend John Fowler visited me on many weekends at the hospital, lacing his visits with humor and prayers for my health and recovery. Those visits, along with those of friends Bob and Cato Schley, meant the world to me.

My daily grind continued with faint progress peppered with occasional visits by my "Rehab Mentor", Fred Brengel, who caned his way into the gym (after a battle back from hip cancer) to egg me on. "Always give 10% more than the therapists ask of you!" he said. That was invaluable advice, which I endeavored to double at every turn. I've found that Fred's advice applies to life, as well. No wonder he built Johnson Controls into such a successful multi-billion dollar company!

In anticipation of my release from the hospital I was given a day pass to go home. Exhausted after a couple of hours, I collapsed on the couch for a quick nap. I awoke an hour later to a hideous smell. Apparently, our small dog had been making her rounds in our backyard and come across some decomposing animal. In her glee, she ingested the entire thing, then laid on my chest and adoringly looked into my face. It was time to get back to the hospital and to the smell of antiseptics.

Toward the end of my Froedtert stay, my doctor noted the unhealed soft dura on the right side of my head where the bone flap was removed and made a call. Shortly thereafter, an authoratative doctor named Jim Sanger from Plastic Surgery showed up in the rehab department when I was doing exercises. Curiosly, I watched him studying the side of my head then probling around my hip. The doctors discussed covering my skull with either nylon or a donor bone and decided the risk of rejection was too great, preferring the option of using a slice of my own hip to accomplish the mission. Another surgery, and a day later, Dr.

Sanger showed up in my room to remove the staples from my hip. I was instructed to wear a foam rubber helmet for protection. Thereafter, I told my kids to call me either "our hippy" or "butt head". Shortly thereafter Bob and Cato Schley wheeled me around the Froedtert campus on a sight seeing trip – it looked like an escape attempt.

Insurance reared its stern head and dictated my hospital release. I then transferred my allegiance to Sacred Heart Rehabilitation Institute on Milwaukee's East Side, while living at home.

The adjustment to de-institutionalizing from the hospital was fairly traumatic. Gone were the days of my marvelous relationships with the hospital staff. It was time to re-knit with my family. In the ensuing years, it would prove tough on them as I strove to rehab myself. Great family patience is a vital support.

Sacred Heart Rehab Begins

My next stop, Sacred Heart Rehabilitation Institute at St. Mary's hospital, dealt with the total individual – leg, arm, speech and spirit. Each discipline was attacked in coordination with the others, all under the organizational thumb of Dr. Jeffrey Cameron, a humble but intense physiatrist.

My leg and walking was my first and most prolonged point of attack in conjunction with their terrific physical therapists. The first one was Teri Mueller, whom I classified as a marvelously mature flower child. Her ministrations brought a gentle awakening to my muscles. Often at night I laid in bed feeling a light pain in the muscles of my left leg. It wasn't scary, but I found it to be profoundly exciting, a sort of subtle reactivation of my atrophied tissues. Every morning before therapy, I was so excited to attack my walking with her that I had to linger in my bathroom with an intestinal bout. I started charting my walking footage, using that as a daily motivator. After every exhausting morning therapy session with her, I went to mass at the St. Mary's chapel in the lobby of the hospital, invariably falling asleep during the service. After awhile as I came home, I pressed our star baby sitter, Kathy Hansen, into action, drafting her into strapping a gait belt onto me and walking around our house (a mightly 55 feet) or down our block. Anything to increase my mileage! Teri kept at me even, through the arrival of her first child. During her leave, other Sacred Heart therapists filled in. All were fantastic and became like family. I would often see them over the next couple of years, and they followed my progress with great enthusiasm. In early 1998 I drafted our housekeeper to walk around our house interior and thereafter drafted any free family member to walk with me, documenting my progress in a notebook. My first significant session was a mighty 550 feet on January 1, 1998, which I considered outstanding.

A week later I started water walking at our local YMCA pool. My aunt and uncle, Nancy and Dave Glassner, were responsible for getting me into the program (with my therapist's blessings and urgings). During my first day at the pool, I was so pathetically weak and unstable that I fell over as soon as I got into the water! After volunteer Sam Cutler righted me, he helped me cautiously walk with a wheeled commode. Since I was so scared at the prospect of my first day of water walking, I found myself laughing at that irony.

I was still feeling a dull ache in my left leg, especially at night when I went to bed, and I found that feeling to be absolutely marvelous. My muscles were reawakening and beginning to rebuild, giving me sublime feedback in a hummingly low level of pain. Over the next few number of months, that pain became my companion and friend, a signal of progress and terrific feedback of things going well. From that point on I only looked forward and never back..

For positive goals, I began to insert tasks or accomplishments that I would love to tackle and conquer – making the rounds and greeting customers in our restaurants, walking my daughters down the aisle, walking at our farm, hiking, skiing, getting on and off an airplane with ease, gardening and doing aggressive outdoor work. All the while, I obsessed with the negative reinforcement of the nurse who told me I would never walk again.

In my business before I got sick, I was pushing the imperative for continuous improvement, and I saw no reason not to apply that to my attitude and performance at therapy. My goal at each session became to improve to the extent of the thickness of a piece of paper. Taken incrementally it wasn't much, but on a macro scale over a greater period of time it tended to produce the thickness of a phone book. There is every reason to assume that that logic can be applied to every turn and stage of life!

I kept pushing myself – always tallying my progress. On February13, 1998, I scored my record walk at home – almost ¼ mile. Three weeks later I beat that by 700' by walking in the YMCA pool.

I was beginning to settle into an independent mode at the YMCA. No longer was a volunteer having to walk with me or holding me as I walked in the pool. I was getting stronger and more stable, often pushing myself to walk, unassisted, for an hour or more at a time – often pushing my weaker leg. My footage steadily increase as it became easier to beat my previous best. It didn't take me long to collapse for a nap when I got home!

Nights were my time for deep introspection and soul-searching. The house was quiet with everyone in bed and I was alone with my demons. I could almost taste the dragging weight of failure, that pull to stop fighting, retreat to the comfort of my wheelchair and give it all up.

What then, I thought? Be a spectator? A receiver? Life-long wheelchair bound? I had already learned to drill wells of humility and listened to everyone urging "acceptance". That's a tall order, and it may be suitable to a lot of personality types. It didn't fit my Type-A nature, even though I had long ago accepted the fact that my life had shatteringly changed. So my nights were spent digging deep, looking for pockets of energy, enthusiasm and persistence to stay on track with my mission to get myself back together. In April, 1998 I went out to a Chinese restaurant with my wonderfully supportive YPO Forum group, with whom I used to be terrifically active. Barely able to manage the logistics of a wheelchair this time, I relished their good-natured company and was astounded to read my prophetic fortune cookie, "You can undertake and complete anything". The upbeat timing couldn't have been better!

Our Heinemann's restaurant staff had, all along, been terrifically interested in my progress. Many of them interfaced with customers and needed to provide information on my status. I was also concerned that the livelihood of many of our staffers was woven into the tapestry of Heinemann's and indirectly into mine, so I made it a point to begin communicating my status and progress, indirectly figuring I could use it as a motivational tool. Thankfully, my wife, Peggy had jumped into the business for me when I was in the hospital. In late April, 1998, one of my letters maintained that the key to the game is "pushing but not overwhelming". Sound advice even today! Other letters updated our staff on footage or mileage walked, always with an upbeat and positive note.

In early May I reached a terrifying but exhilarating high water mark. Armed with a cane and our baby sitter, I walked down our slightly inclined driveway to the end, then turned around and went back up. In the past I had parked my wheelchair one – half way down to accomplish that same feat. This time, I didn't know whether to holler four letter words, cry or laugh! I kept pushing, and within three weeks I had walked ¼ mile down the street and back -albeit at an agonizingly slow rate. What a sight! A middle-aged, stooped-over formerly hyperactive cripple-on-the-mend, sitter in tow, hesitantly caning down the street. Within two weeks I doubled that – another triumph! At about the same time, our great neighbor and friend Chess Barbatelli began walking me down our driveway and part way down the street. His support meant worlds to me, and that kind of help is crucial to any serious rehab effort.

In mid June, my family took a driving trip and I stayed with the St. Mary's hospital Respite Care program. Since it was part of the hospice unit, I was given marvelous opportunity to appreciate the depth of its staff dedication, as well as to snag any spare staffer for an assisted walk down the hallway. On one occasion, I was walking with a charming and dedicated Russian nurse's aide. At one point, I literally had to stop, as my weaker leg was stuck into exhausted immobility. "Never give up!", I told her, as we continued with my stumbling walk until I barely and finally reached my goal.. Over a year later when I bumped into her in a St. Mary's hallway, she reminded me how important those moments were to her (it turns out, coincidentally, that Winston Churchill used those very words in a famous WWII speech). From that moment on, my enunciated goal to myself and our children was, "Aim high and never give up!"

My physical therapist understood my eagerness to keep progressing, as well as my restlessness with my lack of quicker progress, so in June, 1998, she turned me over to another therapist named Monica Diamond. Nationally known for her work with my type of case, Monica took me on with her quietly upbeat gusto. We agreed that graduating from my wheelchair would be my only goal with no holds barred. Monica's style was to laugh at me when she had me in a particularly difficult, pretzel-like position on a floor mat.

Our weekly sessions were tough, as they had to be. The first time Monica assisted me in walking with a cane was difficult for me. I literally had to sit down at mid-point, overcome with emotion. This was practically my dream – my goal! Monica had the humility and good sense to look away before she got me a celebratory Kleenex. Then more walking...

We moved on from there. Every session brought new surprises. For awhile we walked stairs together (hopeless a while ago!), always alert for someone else's thumping of hurried feet on a mission – almost like my old self. Occasionally when I did attempt to hurry I was all feet and as clumsy as a newborn. Our laughs echoed through the St. Mary's stairwells like those of maniacs. When the weather was pleasant we hit the grass circle in front of the hospital. Replete with potholes and dirt bumps, it proved daunting. I felt and looked like Frankenstein reborn. To boot, since this section of the hospital was a sanitarium many years ago, I looked like an escapee from a padded cell. I really didn't care how stupid I looked, however. I already knew humility, and if I fell, at least I would be falling on grass.

On a blustery day kissed with a drop or two of driving rain, Monica thought it was time for me to cross the busy street in front of the hospital. Even though I used a cane and she was with me (only occasionally laughing), it was a clumsy affair doing a gangly rush job to beat two lanes of traffic. Luckily we encountered a lot of patient drivers, and I caught myself wishing for a red-tipped cane equipped with optional begging cup. Underneath the same street connecting Sacred Heart to St. Mary's hospital was a tunnel which provided a safer but less frenetic crossing of the street. While using my wheelchair in the past I had developed the habit of attending mass at the St. Mary's chapel with a wonderfully tight-knit group. En route via the tunnel I encountered many of the same hospital staffers every week as they hustled back and forth on predetermined schedules, always with that furrowed look of medical intensity. Most gave me a cursory nod as they went by, always avoiding my eyes. As I progressed and graduated from my wheelchair to a quad cane and then a single cane, they opened up. It was absolutely electrifying and energizing to see them at eye level – to see the twinkle in their eyes! My progress took on the stamp of new meaning.

In late 1999 my dreams began to be realized. Monica started me walking sans cane during my therapy sessions! I looked a felt like a variety of movie and cartoon characters, from a ganglyIchabod Crane to a silly self-powered dipping drinking bird toy to a spastic preying mantis. What a sight as we wobbled down the Sacred Heart halls – me, bobbing and weaving with her hands on my unsteady hips! She would keep up her editorial comments like, "nice knee!", or "You're dipping again!", occasionally leavening them with a light laugh or a grand guffaw (usually muted when I messed up). It wasn't easy, and I had to reach soul-deep to find courage to keep up my reserves to stay at it and not give up. By Spring, 2000, it got a tad easier, but not easy.

At every therapy session, my hope and dream was for my therapist to let go and to walk solo, much like the way we all learned to ride our bikes when we were kids. In retrospect, rather, each walk led to incremental improvements in strength instead of quantum leaps.

In April, 2000, I went to a Healing mass, my second in two years. I had developed the habit of praying morning and night, along with my weekly trip to mass at St. Mary's chapel when I went to therapy, and I believe prayer is essential to a sound rehab program. Being prayed over in the mass was a literally touching and daunting experience – even humbling. I didn't throw away my cane on the spot, but hoped for longer term progress.

Over a period of time, mainly because I had been a patient at Sacred Heart for two years, I rotated through all of the therapists and got to know all of them quite well. They, in turn, got to know about my positive and type-A attitude, mainly on a gossiping basis. We became friends and I began to regard them as family, readily and eagerly sharing in their poignant moments. My greatest joy was having them note my progress. What fun when they saw my graduation from wheelchair to quad cane, then to single cane! And what deep, rich satisfaction to hear their praise for my lumbering down the hall without a cane during my therapy sessions with Monica. If anything reinforced my fierce desire to walk again, that rewarding praise was most thoroughly successful. It became a critical part of my emotional bank account. During a hip building exercise in late April, 2000, I fell two times on the exercise mat. I was horribly chagrined and carried that sense of failure through the evening and into the next morning. Logically and repeatedly I told myself that is the price of progress, and I told my therapist that my only response was to simply repeat the exercises the following week with the added determination to succeed. I did, probably on the account of patience and persistence (probably two of the most critical dimensions to successful rehab.)

The support of family and friends is essential to any successful rehab effort. One needs them and their encouragement every step of the way in order to win the game.

My oldest son gave me a Progress Book for Christmas and, in

retrospect, his logic was sound. The idea of setting up such a book is terrific. It's a great way to force yourself to positively reinforce forward motion in rehab! Or in life, come to think of it...

Exactly four years after my coma-inducing bout with meningitis, I returned to my Burgundy wine society group for another black tie dinner. This time I limped in with a cane to a standing ovation. The evening marked a special triumph for me because of what I had been through in the ensuing time. Those close to me, and many at the dinner who had hung in with me and prayed for me through my battle and fight back, made the evening particularly special and poignant. In the four years since I was stricken and effectively paralyzed, I figure I walked close to two hundred miles, many of them measured in steps of inches – all of them humbly and slowly wrought, forged with soul-searching and patience from defeat.

Christy

My first Occupational Therapist at Sacred Heart was an upbeat,

sparkling brunette who celebrated life as she worked her way

through it. Christy Niemec was an architypical star therapist,

well-schooled and trained, who broadcast pragmatic hope, laced

with humorous can-do feedback, to all of her patients. We hit it

off immediately, and I found her methodology and approach to be

most fetching. Often, when the therapy gym was crammed with

patients and therapists, we would take our session to the

biofeedback room. Equipped with therapy table, it had everything the gym had, only more privacy. Despite that, our roars of laughter (and her signature explosively twinkly guffaw) could be heard down the hallway. All knew who was in therapy with whom.

Christy was the first therapist to tell me, with softly sympathetic eyes, that there was only so much that she as a therapist could do to help me. The rest was in God's hands. It was difficult to adequately express my gratitude to her. In response to her query about a romantic classical CD for her husband, I reflected, then recommended Rachmaninoff's Symphony #2. I even threw my thanks into my culinary repertoire, inventing Pasta Christy for her. Hopefully, her husband found it palatable.

I would often see Christy across the therapy gym in a treatment session, and her look conveyed humor, warmth, professionalism and a league of profound feelings. A perfect Irishwoman!

On December 21, 1997, Christy was driving with her baby when a truck lost control of its brakes and hit her. She was immediately rushed to the Froedtert hospital NICU. In depressed desperation I called Glenn Meyer to ask him to keep an eye on her in Intensive Care, but he was frantically busy in surgery and we missed one another. Christy's brain herniated at 5:00 on Christmas Day, and she was pronounced dead the following day.

The P's of Successful Rehab – And Successful Life!

1) POSITIVE ATTITUDE– Critical! Always attack

everything in an upbeat, energetic manner. Give off

excess energy because of your attitude. Don't be the type

of person who drains it – a leech! Attack! Win! Set high,

achievable, realistic goals and celebrate their success.

Make certain each therapy session, or each day, improves

you by the thickness of piece of paper. That's not much,

but think about how that adds up with 10 or 100 or

1000!!! My Francophile friend Jim Taylor summed it up in French with "Petite a Petite" (little by little)!

2) PUSH – NEVER STOP! Most people give up. Many quit. Don't ever! Keep looking forward, never back. AIM HIGH AND NEVER GIVE UP!

3) PRAY – Keep up a good relationship with God. Talk with Him. Share your frustrations. Ask for help every day with every therapy session. Thank Him for each successful day, therapy and each bit of progress that you see. You need Him to make it!

4) PEOPLE – You must be surrounded by supportive family and friends in order to keep your efforts underscored and on track, to ease your defeats and help you celebrate your victories. Picture a football game. Your rehab job is the home team on the big field, and you're playing the Big Game. You've got to win it – yard by yard. Your family and finds are the cheerleader and the crowd. Win the

game! Listen to the crowd!

5) PLAY – Never lose your spirit of playfulness and your sense of occasional childlike wonder at life – it helps you! Don't forget to laugh at yourself and never take yourself too seriously.

6) PULL – Help others along. Give them the benefit of your experience and enthusiasm. Move them ahead and counsel them. Pass along your acquired knowledge and wisdom. Give them a chance to win, especially if you did!

7) PASSION – Go at your therapy mission with gusto! How about life, as well?

8) PATIENCE AND PERSISTENCE – We all need to get up, brush off the dust from our fall, take a deep breath, count to ten and go at it again. Maybe again...

A Interesting Thought...

I had just finished walking two miles in the YMCA pool one summer morning and was feeling smugly important. I was the hard-charging, positive and personally pushy member of my group, and things had been going well. As I looked up at the diving board at the end of the pool, I noticed a boy with a positively radiant expression on his face. He would continuously jump off the board, swim to the end of the pool, get out of the water and get back on the board, then repeat the process. I was rocked when I realized that he had no left leg and was missing one-third of his left arm. For over three years, I had been grudgingly battling a slow and atrophied left leg and arm. Geeze – was I embarrassed!

Pain

It has always bothered me when people complain ad nauseum and demand attention for life's bumps in the road. I've always tended to underplay things, and I found during my ordeal that I generally have a very high threshold for pain.

The pain from my meningitis was consuming, as was the agony from my three subsequent brain surgeries.

How did I cope? Many asked me this question. Drugs helped, but they tended to get nasty and addictive. Prayer was a great aid, and I stoutly believe that we need the loving help of God to get through incredible times like I witnessed. One priest even suggested that I picture myself on the cross with Jesus, sharing His pain.

Each of us, some day, will have our days in the unique, murky world that true pain presents. Dealing with it properly, I found, is really a matter of mixing art with craft.

My meningitis affected the layer of tissue (meninges) that was directly inside my skull and then went deeper. Strokes occur farther inside the brain, taking different dimension than meningitis.

As I did research into meningitis and its complexities, I increasingly came across material on strokes, which many experts regard as a kissing cousin.

Where as my problem was caused by a surgical mishap, strokes are a different game that is both fascinating and challenging. They are discouraging, painful and daunting. Additionally, they can be energizing or enriching. Literally, you can find your recovery can lead you to know that the sky can be your limit.

Again, as Winston Churchill Said, "Never Give In"!

Part 2:

Strokes

Where the willingness is great, the difficulties cannot be great.

-Machiavelli (1469-1527)

Stroke – The Real Thing

Recently, I was dining at a busy restaurant near a table occupied by a friend and his nephew. After about one-half hour, I heard quietly panicked voices of diners around his table. When I made my way over, I noticed my friend, rigid, staring straight ahead. He didn't react to nearly panicky interest, and I heard someone yelling to call an ambulance. Knowing that many ambulances tend to take stroke patients to the nearest hospital, which in this case was good but not great, I sternly but gently told his nephew to take him to our Level 1 trauma center hospital sans ambulance.

After his arrival at the hospital and his reception by their 24/7

stroke team, he was admitted to their neuro intensive care unit.

Three days later, he was immersed in their rehab program. Today,

he is home free and is one happy camper!

Causes and Signs of a Stroke

According to many sources, poor blood flow to the brain results in cell death. Two types of such death are common:

1) Ischemic, due to lack of blood flow.
2) Hemorrhagic, due to bleeding in various degrees.

Symptoms include problems with speaking, dizziness, loss of vision on one side, atrial fibrillation or some degree of paralysis on one side. Some people report headaches in varying degrees.

If the above last less than two hours, it is dubbed a 'mini stroke'.

The primary and basic causes of a stroke are:

- High blood pressure

- Tobacco use

- Diabetes

- Previous stroke history

- Poor eating habits (e.g. too much fat)

What Hospital Should You Hit?

If someone is displaying signs of a stroke, many ambulances tend to take them to the nearest hospital. DON'T ALLOW THAT! Someone you know should, without delay, be taken to a Level One Trauma Center with a 24/7 dedicated stroke team composed of neurologists, radiologists and neurosurgeons. If it's a teaching hospital with a depth of talent, so much the better. That way, dedicated professionals can properly diagnose and treat any patient correctly, making the difference between life and death and proper rehabilitation relatively simple. Lesser hospitals aren't properly equipped and staffed to intervene in a critical issue like a stroke.

Common Side Effects of Stroke

Some patients have profound weakness or one-sided non function (called hemi-paralysis) in which one side of the body practically totally dominates the other side. Often, the side on the opposite side of the brain attack side is affected. A panoply of therapeutic treatments are needed to attempt to right the wrongs of the stroke.

Subluxation (or dropped) shoulders and seemingly near separation from the shoulder are often noted. Some therapists design exercises to minimize the problem by strengthening the shoulder muscles.

Depression and generally mixed moods can be common. Some patients also experience sensitivity to noise and to exaggerated emotional circumstances. Bawling at emotional movies can be most awkward, as well as hysterical (almost maniacal) laughter at others. These mood swings can almost look like a manic-depressive challenge:

- Impatience with yourself or others
- Tiredness, often to the point of frequent naps.
- Headaches in varying degrees
- Lack of focus. A book like this can take many months.

Diagnosis and Treatment

71

Immediately, a twenty-four hours per day, seven days per week team of well-trained neurologists, neuroradialogists and neurosurgeons will provide an emergency MRI, or CI Scan, or both, to map the location and the cause of the stroke. Using their advanced imagery, they will also check on the complexity of the condition as well as other neurovascular conditions like raised cranial (head) pressure or aneurysms. It is critically important to only get treatment by a first class, nationally known facility, not a lesser one.

Ischemic strokes, the most common, occur when an artery is blocked. The FDA has approved the most widely known and used drugs, called thrombolytic (or clot-busters) that can stop ischemic strokes. This TPA can actually reverse a stroke. For use since 1996, it can be highly effective if safely administered.

If a patient arrives too late for treatment via TPA, some doctors opt for endovascular procedures performed inside the blocked vessels to remove the clot.

Next comes a stay in the hospital, which may vary from a couple of days to months. At that time, a physiatrist (physical doctor) will evaluate a patient and prescribe treatment to a team of therapists. Treatments can be in-house for a period, followed by a post-discharge set of treatments by an outpatient program or a home treatment arrangement that suits the patient. Here is where attitude, patience and persistence come into the picture.

"Practice is the best of all instructors"

Publilius Syrus (42 BC)

Starting out with Physical Therapy (PT)

Physical therapy (PT) usually starts in the hospital with doctor (physiatrist) evaluation and referral. A good therapist will ferret out details of the patient's previous life to determine a baseline of prospective functions and goals. Evaluation of movement and determining each patient's positives and negatives through careful observation helps greatly in setting goals with each patient. Treatment and attitudes should be positive, not negative. (One doesn't have a 'bad leg' or 'bad hip' – it should always be called 'weaker leg and stronger leg' or 'weaker hip and stronger hip' –

huge difference and a fire-able offense. One's PT should establish a point-by-point progress goal plan. Sometimes, a wheelchair may be needed for proper mobility although I use a scooter. For stability, devices like a walker, quad cane or cane work out well. For added walking stability, a number of PTs like to encourage a leg splint (many are removable) or an AFO (ankle foot orthotic) that is sometimes jointed at the ankle to mimic normal foot movement.

The PT will follow progress and alter goals as needed, keeping the patient as active as possible, always focusing on positive, not negative progress. If ones goals are met, one's PT will determine whether the patient should be discharged or transitioned into an outpatient or home exercise program.

As always, the Big Gorilla called health insurance a critical factor, unless the patient has just robbed Fort Knox.

Some enlightened doctors and therapists have had great success with constraint induced movement therapy, wherein a patient's strong arm is in some form bound, forcing the subject to use the weaker arm. Neuroplasticity can take over quickly as the weaker cells in your brain "learn" from the stronger ones.

Neuro PT

Simply put, neuro PT is therapy administered by specialists trained in dealing with people who have neurological diagnoses such as stroke and brain injury. The therapist is trained in and certified in Neuro Development treatment (NDT, as they fondly call it).

The NDT trained PT will help to facilitate correct movement and positioning depending on the extent of stroke damage. NDT involves more visits and more time than regular PT. When one is doing outpatient NDT therapy, more complexity is usually

involved. Patience and persistence never hurts, either.

Neuroplasticity

For years, conventional wisdom held that after a stroke, one's essential physical functions faced "game over" time. Now, that game is over.

Strokes or huge brain-damaging incidents like meningitis can actually lead the brain to rewire itself even with older brain cells. Our brain cells have a plastic nature – if one cell is damaged, another younger cell can sometimes take its place, learning from the older one. Sometimes, if a patient cannot walk, resourceful physicians and therapists can teach him or her how to crawl, much as a baby does, before tentatively trying to walk. Many scientists feel the brain can reprogram itself after devastating setbacks like strokes.

The average adult has one hundred billion neurons, many of which can communicate with one another in order to pass along function. The famous actor Christopher Reeve (Superman), was able to partially recover via neuorplasticity seven years after his accident. Sigmund Freud began his career as a neuroscientist. Pablo Casals, the brilliant cellist, was asked why he continued to practice. His response, "I was making progress"

In experiments with rats, enriched activities increase overall brain weight by 10%. Even debilitating diseases like Alzheimer's can be delayed by spending time rebuilding an active brain. At some point in the future, we may be able to build and repair "broken" brains, replacing them with more vibrant ones. There is no guarantee of a total recovery, but research shows that even a partial repair is possible. This spells optimism and great news for the estimated more than 400,000 potentially vibrant people who are admitted to hospitals with head injuries or strokes. The trillions of neurological "switches" frequently interacting in the average brain may have some hope.

The quality of a person's life is in direct proportion to their commitment to excellence

Vince Lombardi

Occupational Therapy (OT)

By definition, Occupational Therapy (OT) helps develop, recover

or maintain meaningful activities (some therapists name this

ADLs, or Activities of Daily Life). OTs must be well-schooled,

often at a university, and they need to work closely in a team

effort with other therapists in successful rehab. On the trivia side,

OT practices started as early as 100 BC and were refined with

time. Properly implemented, it can even help with the physical and mental health of patients, increasing one's quality of life.

It is better to deal by speech than by letter

Bacon (1561-1626)

Speech Therapy (ST)

Years ago, conventional wisdom dictated that speech therapy, especially, seeks to reconnect the brains cells, encouraging the resumption of proper functioning. As of 2018, it's more than that.

Speech therapy is more than adjusting and enhancing a subject's speaking ability. Rather, it is a set of disciplines that can, when linked, ultimately result in reconnection, and then some. Current "tricks of the speech therapy trade" include:

— Word-finding drills, including definitions

- Memory improvement
- Problem-solving drills that encourage mental processing and organizational development
- Reading comprehension and memory
- Sentence structure and learning

Tip – since a stroke can occasionally affect one side of the body, the other side can be adversely affected and, in some cases, partially paralyzed. Many patients complain of partial face weakness which can affect speech, enunciation and, in some cases, drooling. Yikes-what an embarrassment!

To help address this by strengthening your facial muscles, look in your mirror and make a variety of exaggerated faces like lip puckering, cheek moving, eye winking or forehead raising. Good for parties or trick-or-trick time...

I recently met a very intelligent and talented person who, after suffering through a brutal stroke, can easily follow conversation but cannot easily vocalize an appropriate response. Another therapy issue...

The Importance of Exercise

Don't sit in your chair feeling sorry for yourself! Involve yourself in a personal training program. Some can be held at rehab facilities and others are available through your YMCA or other resources.

Recent studies in Japan and in the US indicated that ten minutes of light but sustained exercise per day will improve your mood.

If possible, try to make certain that each program involves other people, especially those with your type of challenge, because socialization is good for all concerned – you're in this together.

Water or pool programs are especially great, since the water provides minor resistance and builds muscles uniformly. As noted above, you will feel better...

Botox-Not just for Hollywood

Some post-stroke patients experience stiffness (called "tone" in the trade) which can limit function and affect therapy as well as daily functioning. Many physiatrists (physical doctors, not psychiatrists) find the following to be helpful:

- Baclofen tablets, taken during the day and/or at night.

- Exercise to overcome tight muscles

- Baclofen pump- an implanted small metal pump which delivers targeted baclofen at a variable rate directly to the spinal cord. After your surgeon installs it, it may be adjusted as needed, then refilled every one to six months. Usually the entire pump must be replaced every five to seven years.

— Botox or Xeomin (cheaper option that was available as of approximately 2015) uses carefully targeted injections to relieve tone or stiffness in one's chest, arms, hands and/or legs for approximately three months. Usually, it takes a week or two to be effective with maximum impact within one month. Logically, if patient's tight muscles are loosened, movement is easier and/or other muscles can be used to take up some of the slack, "training" them to be stronger or more effective.

As a side note, many doctors prefer Xeomin ("zee-o-men" or "zeemen") depending upon the doctor, and insurance coverage.

Yours is the Earth and everything that's in it, And – which is more
you'll be a man, my son!

Kipling

A hard beginning maketh a good ending

John Heywood (1497-1580)

Cell me!

Significant research is being done on possible stem cell therapy to help with stroke recovery. Interested in the approximately 800,000 strokes happening per year in the US, Professor Gary Steinberg at Stanford University has done extensive research on the feasability of injecting adult stem cells into one's brain that has been most affected by the stroke. Some patients could readily go from a wheelchair to walking, to using arm/hand and to improve speech. Extensive research is continuing in the neuroscience field to plum the full potential of this concept.

In some cases as recently as 2018, "SB623 cells" are taken from the bone marrow of donors and are modified to boost brain function. Bone marrow represents 4% of one's total body mass and it produces 500 billion cells per day. What wondrous potential that in 2018 has been petitioned to congress to actively fund research!

Shake it up – Seizures, etc.

As an unfortunate consequence of strokes, meningitis or head injuries, some people have to sadly deal with the incidence of seizures occasionally or frequently. A number of health professionals prescribe drugs such as anticonvulsants: Depakote, neurontin, keppra, tegretol, topamax.

If drugs aren't enough, some doctors recommend a gadget called VNS, or vagus nerve stimulator. Attached to the left vagus nerve in one's neck, leading to the brain, it originates in a generator that is surgically implanted in the chest during an outpatient procedure by a specially trained neurosurgeon. An outpatient procedure, it usually takes less than an hour under mild sedation, followed by its initial activation. Afterwards the VNS unit periodically sends precise electrical pulses to the brain, often short-circuiting a seizure. Periodically a patient will visit a neurological VNS specialist who will monitor the unit and adjust the pulses intensity and frequency. The patient usually carries a small magnet that, when "swiped" across the outside of the skin covering the three inch VNS unit will short-circuit or stop an early onset or full seizure. The VNS unit contains a high-tech battery that will deliver six-plus years of performance. Often, it is so effective that one's neurologist can safely juggle or even lessen one's seizure drug usage, lessening side effects. As a minor side effect, its "firing" can cause minor throat irritation and throat clearing. Some patients tell friends that it is a consequence of allergies. Many patients call the VNS a minor miracle.

Thou hast seen nothing yet.

Cervantes (1547-1616)

Planning and Goal Setting

This section is not rocket science. It always makes sense in your life, especially in your comeback, to set planning goals for yourself.

For example:

Where do you want to be in x-amount of time? What will you or your progress look like? Make sure you set reasonable targets, rather than flying to the moon. List each of your targets or goals on a separate piece of paper.

Allowing plenty of room for each goal that you commit to paper, list what details will derail you or prevent you from reaching each goal.

Next, list a reasonable date to accomplish each target. It's better to decide on a longer term goal rather than a shorter length goal (Rome wasn't built in a day, etc). Make sure that each target is easy to attack and achieve. If you need help (a doctor, a therapist, an assistance, etc) add that to your "accomplish" date. It will work, but you will sometimes have to be patient with yourself!

Problem Solving

Let's say that, in your battle to achieve your goals or in your daily life, you run into a road block, a problem that gets in the way.

Attack it! Follow this effective approach:

Using separate pieces of legal pad – sized paper, list the problems with which you must contend. Titles may be patience, walking, thinking coherently, talking or arm function.

Next, list what is getting in the way of accomplishing the solution for each problem.

In addition, list a feasible date or time frame that will successfully indicate your defeat of your challenge.

Last, list a minor occasion or event to celebrate your accomplishment!

As the kids say today, "Rock on!".

You're Fired!

In 2018, it was revealed that the CEO of a regional hospital chain was paid $1,500,000.00 PER MONTH!! That rivals the lottery or a run at Monte Carlo. The medical field is highly structured, sometimes to the benefit of some and to the detriment of the struggling patient.

Many medical organizations, like their corporate counterparts, are "top down", where highly paid top title holders preside over the top of the health care pyramid. Next come layers of a well-intentioned bureaucracy (government, anyone?). Finally, at the base of this gigundo pyramid and, after the able doctors and therapists, are the struggling, financially – challenged patients, It's all wrong, and it should be upended with the patient at the base feeding into the quagmire of the hospital corporation and ending up with the CEO who should be the cheerleader.

Or-picture a doughnut of health care. The patient should be at the center of this marvelous pastry, surrounded by able therapists, support staff, doctors and management.

Health care should always be patient-centered. If not, fire those who get in the way! In my experience with my comeback, I've parted ways with over a dozen therapists and doctors. With each new one I hired, we clearly discussed my needs and their abilities and an action plan. That way, we all win!

Where does God fit in?

We are in God's hand

Shakespeare (1564-1616)

"To see how high! -

It reaches up

To God's blue sky!"

John Oxenham (1861-1941)

There is no better friend and ally in your struggle than God. As you begin each day, wake up with God and ask Him for company and guidance for the day. Before each therapy session or appointment, ask the Big Guy for hand-holding and strength. Get in the habit after your day or meeting to thank Him for support and guidance.

And, at the risk of sounding corny, ask Him to hold you in His arms when you go to bed. Maybe you'll find a hint of comfort and guidance when you awake!

If you're the least big religious, start up a "comeback" relationship with the Big Guy. Pray daily for progress in your healing and rehab and seek comfort in God's arms. Practice (even force) patience with yourself or others. And, seek fortitude to stick it out and thrive in the long run. A healthy dose of humility doesn't hurt, either...

A Quiet Thought

During a recent silent retreat, which was almost impossible for me, I ran into a terribly crippled young Hispanic man. We took a heretical moment to whisper about his life and direction. Jose told me that some of the best doctors have tried to help him to no avail, as have some of the best therapists. He, despite his best efforts, cannot bring himself back.

His only solution, he whispered to me, is totally trusting in God. Amen, Jose, go with God. And may all of you go with God, as well!

Therapy on Steroids

Link up with a key placement person at a local therapy-related university. For twenty-two years, grad OT and PT students were invaluable to me. I regarded them as fertile, educational resources and they probably viewed me as a sort of "lab rat" on whom to sharpen their skills. Additionally, these wonderful and enthusiastic pre-professionals were invaluable with shopping errands and help (even typing this manuscript). A perfect win-win.

What thought can think, another thought can mend, look home.

Robert Southwell (1561-1595)

Key Recovery Aids

Practice Moderation – avoid extremes: Forbear resenting injuries as much as you think they deserve.

Display Tranquility – Be not disturbed at trifles nor at accidents, common or unavoidable.

Prevention of Future Strokes

— As is the case in many health obstacles, practice moderation in all things, including eating habits.

— Actively involve your doctor in your life. With him or her, designate a hospital for stroke treatment and involve your key friends or family in your decision.

— Many doctors advise patients to take 1 mg of aspirin daily. Some doctors consider medicines such as melagatran, cilostratzol, blood thinners (warfarin or its equivalents) or direct xa inhibition.

— Involve your family in your case. Teach them how to clearly recognize another stroke and what to do or where to go for help.

It's all in how You Look at it.

Many people separate from another with the parting note, "Take Care". How negative! It implies that the greetee are about to get steamrolled or shot to pieces.

Instead try the positive track, saying "Have a terrific day!" or "Have fun today!"

What a tremendous difference!

A Hard Beginning Maketh a Good Ending.

John Heywood

The Importance of Family and Friends

Form an invincible army of protective and supportive friends, linked up with positive family support, and you will be fortified to attack most obstacles with positive energy. They can protect you with caring, help forge your goals and pump their fists at whatever success you achieve. Truly, they will add tremendous meaning to your life!

"He plants trees to benefit another generation"

Cecilius Statius (220-168 BC)

Moving On

I hope my own experience with menintits was a tad hlpful to you – at least it is probably good for insomnia.

Occasionally, another stroke may rear its ugly head. Regardless, in the future, ALWAYS have access to a level one trauma center, not a lesser local hospital. The level one center must have a 24/7 (twenty-four hour per day, seven days per week) stroke team on duty.

When buying a house or condo, or moving into an apartment, insist on a location near the stroke center. Even when traveling, it's wise to do your homework and locate near a top – notch hospital, rather than relying on a dusty clinic with rusty needles and monosyllabic staffing.

After your stroke, your suffering, recovery and rehab, you can do one of two things:

1) Sit in one spot and stare at the wall, doing little and bemoaning the fact that life hasn't been fair to you or to those around you.

2) Look inside for inner strength, determination and properly organized planning plus use goal setting to mount a concerted attack on reclaiming and advancing your life. What an opportunity!

Above all, dial your psyche into a positive and permanent mindset to conquer all adveristy that interrupts your life and threatens to derail you. It's all in your attitude, and you can do it!

"The human body is an instrument for the production of art in the life of the human soul"

Alfred North Whitehead (1861-1947)

Power of Medical Care Attorney

This is critical for all of us – always. Identify one or two individuals with whom you are close. Honestly discuss your physical condition, your treatment wishes, and your preference for serious illness or end-or-life actions. Would you like to be put in a nursing home if things look tough? If your condition is serious enough that if death could be imminent and you are approaching or are in a potentially life-ending coma, would you like treatment to cease or would you like to be "unplugged"?

Fill out your POMCA form, available from many doctors, hospitals, lawyers, or on the web, and give copies to all parities involved in your life and/or death.

Here's to your Comeback.

Cheers, and forge on!

John Burns

With recognition, thanks and appreciation:

- Froedtert and the Medical College of Wisconsin

- Concordia University of Wisconsin

- Familiar Quotations, John Bartlett, 1955

- Brain Plasticity and Behavior, Bryan Kolb (1947-), University of Cambridge, Lawrence Elbaum Assoc. & Publishers, Mahwah, NJ

- Kerry McVey, graduate Physical Therapy student, Concordia University of Wisconsin, for her unbounded enthusiasm and professional typing. She'll go far!

- Monica Diamond PT, MS, NCS, C/NDT. Board Certified Neurologic Clinical Specialist, Outpatient Neuro and Brain Injury Day Programs. Ascension/Sacred Heart Rehab Institute. 2323 N. Lake drive, Milwaukee, WI 53211. Note: Monica is not only talented, but is gaining national and international popularity – deservedly so.

- To my son, Father John, for his sagacity and help in publishing this.

- To Peggy Burns for her editing skills.

- Dr. Jeffrey S. Cameron, Physiatrist, Sarasota, FL